# ALZHEIMER'S CHRONICLES: WHEN THE PAST IS NOT PRESENT

## Poetry Memoir by Ann Holmes

# ALZHEIMER'S CHRONICLES: WHEN THE PAST IS NOT PRESENT

*Dear Hal and Thelma,
This is what has been happening to us!
Love, Ann*

# ALZHEIMER'S CHRONICLES:
# WHEN THE PAST IS NOT PRESENT

Copyright © 2017 Ann Holmes.

All rights reserved. No part of this book may be used or reproduced by any means, graphic, electronic, or mechanical, including photocopying, recording, taping or by any information storage retrieval system without the written permission of the author except in the case of brief quotations embodied in critical articles and reviews.

iUniverse books may be ordered through booksellers or by contacting:

iUniverse
1663 Liberty Drive
Bloomington, IN 47403
www.iuniverse.com
1-800-Authors (1-800-288-4677)

Because of the dynamic nature of the Internet, any web addresses or links contained in this book may have changed since publication and may no longer be valid. The views expressed in this work are solely those of the author and do not necessarily reflect the views of the publisher, and the publisher hereby disclaims any responsibility for them.

Any people depicted in stock imagery provided by Thinkstock are models, and such images are being used for illustrative purposes only.
Certain stock imagery © Thinkstock.

ISBN: 978-1-5320-3396-4 (sc)
ISBN: 978-1-5320-3397-1 (e)

Print information available on the last page.

iUniverse rev. date: 01/13/2018

Jack Holmes

Also by Ann Holmes

*Shards* (Turn of River Press, 2004)

*A Leaf Called Socrates* (iUniverse, 2011)

*A Play of Mirrors* (iUniverse, 2016)

**Ann Holmes,** poet and painter, lives in Ann Arbor, Michigan. She attended Bennington College and received her Bachelor of Arts degree from Sarah Lawrence College. After earning her Doctorate of Arts degree in art education from New York University, she returned to Sarah Lawrence for an MFA degree in poetry. *When The Past Is Not Present: Alzheimer's Chronicles,* is Holmes' fourth poetry memoir. Her poetry has been published by *Poetry Magazine Online, Asian Pacific Journal, Connecticut River Review* and other journals.

# Acknowledgments

Grateful acknowledgement to the editors of 3rd Wednesday where my poem "His Last Days Driving" was published.

I thank my artist sister, Jane Mason, who drew my husband as part of her Starbucks series of sketch books. It is the perfect cover for my book.

I am also grateful to Stefan Petrmichl who formatted the manuscript and PhotoShopped the interior photograph of my husband. With his technical expertise and discriminating eye, he perfected the spacing for my free form poems. I thank him for his patience throughout revisions.

Many thanks to Don Postema for his beautiful review.

I am grateful to Lisa Bessette for proofreading my manuscript.

I thank my daughter Megan Holmes, my son Kip Holmes, my sister Jane Mason, and friends Jane Bridges, Brunie Barber, Sylvia Clark, Zdena Heller, Dassie Hoffman, Joyce Plummer, Amee Weis and Rose Wilson who read some of these poems as I was writing them.

Last of all, I could not have done this the book without "the Old Man," my husband, who unwittingly served as my protagonist.

The poem of the mind...has not always had to find: the scene was set...It repeated what was in the script...It has to construct a new stage...an invisible audience listens, not to the play, but to itself...The poem of the act of the mind.

    Wallace Stevens,
    Of Modern Poetry, 1940

# ALZHEIMER'S CHRONICLES: WHEN THE PAST IS NOT PRESENT

# Table of Contents

## Part 1

| | |
|---|---|
| A Stranger to Himself | 1 |
| Reading the *Times* | 2 |
| Life Changes | 3 |
| His Last Days Driving | 4 |
| Moving Out | 5 |
| Moving In | 6 |
| Room without a View | 7 |
| A Little Incident | 8 |
| A Cup of Tea | 9 |
| OCD | 10 |
| Where Are You? | 11 |
| Gone | 12 |
| My Nightmare | 13 |
| His Nightmare | 14 |
| Who's on First? | 15 |
| You Nod Off | 16 |
| Unexpected Memory | 17 |
| Almost No Memory | 18 |
| Believe It or Not | 19 |
| *Little Miss Sunshine* | 20 |

| | |
|---|---|
| Oops | 21 |
| Burma Shave | 22 |
| Breakdown | 23 |
| Worry Time | 24 |
| Brrr | 25 |
| A Necklace of Words | 26 |
| Something/Nothing | 27 |
| A Joke He Loves to Tell | 28 |
| Day after Day | 29 |
| Expectations | 30 |
| Getting It Right | 31 |
| Ready Made | 32 |
| Metamorphosis | 33 |
| Quandary | 34 |
| Each Morning | 35 |

# Part 2

| | |
|---|---|
| How It Happened | 39 |
| Déjà Vu | 40 |
| The Time Comes | 41 |
| First Day | 42 |
| Three Monkeys[0000 | 43 |
| Now and Then | 44 |
| Interpretation | 45 |

| | |
|---|---|
| When I Least Expect It | 46 |
| Odd | 47 |
| The Good News | 48 |
| Phone Call | 49 |
| Broken Record | 50 |
| Manuela | 51 |
| Half a Sandwich | 52 |
| Manuela is Told the Truth | 53 |
| Just Kidding | 54 |
| Identity Theft | 55 |
| Enigma | 56 |
| Fun House Mirror | 57 |

# Notes

# Introduction

I ask, *how do you know it's Alzheimer's?*
The neurologist says,

> *if it looks like a duck,*
> *swims like a duck,*
> *quacks like a duck,*
> *walks like a duck,*
> *then it probably is a duck.*

It took me fifty-four poems
to try and discover
what Alzheimer's is.

Each poem is a piece of that puzzle.

# Part 1

# A Stranger to Himself

It is a major achievement
for my husband,
whose business took him
all over the world,

to the middle east
before it fell apart,
before he fell apart,

to pick up the phone
and take a message.

Or if he happens
to jot down a name
on a scrap of paper,
he hasn't a clue
where he put it.

## Reading the *Times*

He has something urgent
to tell her. She wants to listen,
but not now, not in the middle
of a Maureen Dowd editorial.

Instead he addresses
the goldfinch, perched
on the feeder,
pecking at flax seed:

*Yoyo Ma is coming to
Tanglewood this August.*

It is early March,
much too soon for its
dun colored feathers
to be splotched yellow.

## Life Changes

I first suspected something was seriously wrong
on that last trip to Tanglewood
when I did all the driving.

Before then I thought we'd live
in Connecticut forever.
Before then I thought we'd live
in our house forever.
Before then I thought we'd live
forever.

That was when we stopped
renting the cottage in Martha's Vineyard.
That was when we stopped
taking Metro-North into New York.
That was when we stopped
buying tickets to plays and concerts.

That was when he stopped
taking books out of the library.
That was when he stopped
weeding the garden.
That was when he stopped
feeding the birds.

# His Last Days Driving

I beg and beg
my ancient husband
to stop driving
his ancient jeep.

I beg and beg
my ancient husband
to quit playing Mahler
full blast on the tape deck
of his ancient jeep.

When I hear the cacophony
of heartbreak pull up
into the driveway,
I know he is home.

## Moving Out

Out go my journals, dreams
and ideas that never jelled.

Out goes the old psychic reading,
though some of it did come true.

Out go the blank canvases
I hadn't time to paint.

Out goes my easel, once
owned by a Bauhaus painter.

Out go my pallet and oil paints.
(I'll keep the brushes, just in case.)

Out go hundreds of art postcards.

Will the ghost stuck inside
Auntie Park's portrait
survive the move?

## Moving In

This place is a lot nicer
than the idea of living
in such a place implies.

Some people here
suggest I stash my
overflow of poetry
books inside empty
kitchen cupboards.

I don't know how
Elizabeth Bishop
or Emily Dickinson
will feel about this.

## Room Without a View

The morning after
we move into
Senior Living,

my Connecticut friend
phones and asks:
*what's the view?*

I step over
boxes, half
unpacked,
look out

the living room
bay window at
a parking lot
and an American flag.

## A Little Incident

Our first Sunday morning at
Glacier Hills, we are jolted out of
a deep sleep by the strident voice of
a woman, yelling on her smartphone.

Is this what living in a senior complex is like?

A knock at the door. An aide to collect
emptied boxes. Hearing the racket down below,
she dashes over to our partially open window.
Opens it wider. Shouts down:

*hey Miss Donna, you talking way too loud!*

## A Cup of Tea

This morning I wake with a crick
in my knee. *How about a cup
of tea?* I ask. *Fine,* you say,
waiting for me to make it.

> *How about you
> make me tea?
> Tea bags are
> in the red
>   Christmas
>   tin on the
>    shelf above
>     the sink. Fill
>      two   cups
>       with water.
>       Put a tea
>        bag    in
>       each  cup.
>      Open  the
>     microwave
>     door and
>     put the
>     c u p s
>      inside.
>       Shut it.
>       Punch
>        t h e
>         timer
>           on 2.*

>       *What?*

## OCD

Waking from the earliest
 of his early morning naps,
  the Old Man shuffles into
   his corner of the living room,
    plops himself down into his
     black leather chair, takes out
      his magnifying glass and leans
       forward to examine a stamp
        his granddaughter brought
         back from Paris. And with the
          utmost care, he squirts a blob
           of Elmer's glue onto the back
            of the Île de la Cité stamp he
             pastes onto the very last page.

## Where Are You?

Even when I tell you
where it is I am off to,
and what time
I'm due back,

and write it down
on two sticky notes
I tape onto

the inside
and outside
of our front door,

you ask: *where
are you off to?
What time will
you be back?*

## Gone

is the curiosity
that killed
the cat.

Were you
to see these
fractured
lines I write,

in less than
a minute
you'd forget.

# My Nightmare

*What did you say?* asks the Old Grouch,
wrenching me out of the jaws of my nightmare.

*For God's sake, go back to sleep.
It's three o'clock in the morning!* I shout,
trying to claw my way back into my dream.

In a flood of tears, I am driving the Old Grouch

somewhere deep in the slums
of Mexico, where each shack
is painted sunflower yellow,
raspberry pink or lime jello green,
and every floor slants downhill.

Try as I might, I cannot extract
the Old Grouch from his predicament,
nor will he loosen his grip on my nightmare.

## His Nightmare

He wakes up in a sweat.
He has this new job.
Doing what?
He has no idea.

Where is his attaché case?
Does anyone today
use an attaché case?

What city will he fly out of?
What city will he fly into?

Bomb-sniffing beagles
in little red jackets, find
a black backpack inside
a Newark dumpster.

A bomb explodes.

## Who's on First?

*Is Rise & Shine today?* asks the Old Man.

*Yesterday was Monday,*
  *when we went to Rise*
    *& Shine. T o d a y*
      *is T u e s d a y.*
        *On Tuesday,*
          *we go to*
            *Tai Chi.*
              *Monday,*
               *Wednesday,*
                *and Friday,*
                 *we go to*
                   *R i s e &*
                    *S h i n e*
                   *but since*
                  *tomorrow is*
                 *Wednesday,*
                *c e r t a i n l y*
               *t o m o r r o w*
              *we will be going*
             *to Rise & Shine.*

*Is Rise & Shine today?* asks the Old Man.

## You Nod Off

Your left foot
     twitches in
         your sleep
            and I hear
              you giggle.
            Try as I might,
          I don't know
        the last time
       I caught you
  g i g g l i n g
a w a k e.

## Unexpected Memory

Our kids ask us out
to dinner.

*Whose treat?*
you ask.

Could it be
you remember
way back when

we were young
and so strapped
for money

we'd hold our breath,
till someone else
paid the bill.

## Almost No Memory

Most of the poems I write
are about you.
I don't show them to you
nor do you ask to see them.

I place "Unexpected Memory"
in your hand that used
to guide the tiller
of our daysailer
on Long Island Sound.

You shut your eyes,
"Unexpected Memory"
a phantom jib sheet
in your sailor's hand.

## Believe It or Not

We leave the Saturday night movie, together,
but somehow you, with your brand new blue walker,
are last on the elevator; there is no room for me.

Doors close.
In minutes it's back.
Doors open.

Here, all by itself,
is your brand new blue
walker—but where
are you?

## Little Miss Sunshine

Too late to find two seats together,
we sit a row apart.

These days I so seldom laugh
but tonight I laugh so hard
I don't see you leave.

You find your way back to the apartment.
Change into your pajamas.

Sitting up in bed, you pencil in words
in the easy crossword puzzle paperback
I got you at the Detroit airport.

*Why didn't you wait for me?*
*Why did you leave without me?*

# Oops

On the way to our garden plot,

I say, *wait a minute while
I go get a sweater.*

I come back
to find you
at Carl's plot,

hosing down his tomatoes.

# Burma Shave

The Old Man speaks
to our daughter as if she
were his sister, Nancy:

*Remember when it
took two days
to drive
from St. Louis
to Michigan?*

*How we stopped
right in the middle
of a corn field
if mother
had to go?*

*How you and I
took turns reading
Burma Shave signs?*

# Breakdown

I turn the car key. Nothing happens.
The tow truck comes.
Mid-charge, the battery dies.
My car is towed to a garage.

I am about to head home,
when I catch sight
of a supermarket across the street.
Good—I'm out of everything.

I pull into the nearest handicap space.
In all the hullabaloo, I forgot my cane.
(Don't despair; like any decent sonnet,
the best is yet to come.)

With the temerity of a tightrope walker,
I place one foot in front of the other.

# Worry Time

I used to stop myself
from worrying too much,
by worrying only a little bit
at a time. Then I had this idea,
I'd stop doing Worry Time in my
head and do it on my MacBook Pro,
beginning with the anaphora, what if.

What if I die before he dies?
What if I trip and break my hip?
What if he trips and breaks his hip?

"What if?" stirs up a plethora of bad ideas.
Why not write about when he was shivering,
and I goosed the thermostat up a few degrees.

# Brrr

*It's chilly,* complains the Old Man, shivering.
He walks over to the thermostat.
Squints to read the faint numbers.
It is set at seventy-five.

The Old Man is convinced
he must be as adept
as a rocket scientist to raise
or lower the temperature.

I tiptoe over to the hard to read,
hard to adjust thermostat,
and nudge it up a notch.

## A Necklace of Words

Suddenly I find myself enunciating
each word clearly,
as I'd do for any non-
English language speaker.

Each thought I string
into a necklace
of words.

If I were to say, *time to go to supper,*
he hears, *why do I go to suffer?*

It makes perfect sense
inside his tangled brain.

## Something/Nothing

He claims,
*something
is going on
in the hall.*
*I  h e a r
n o i s e s
out there.*
I  o p e n
the door.
No one
is there.
He says,
*some one
is knocking
at the door*
I  o p e n
the door
w i d e.
No one
there.

## A Joke He Loves to Tell

Whenever Moose Tracks
ice cream is on the menu,
the Old Man asks,

*bet you can't guess
how Moose Tracks
got its name?*

*On a cold snowy day
follow any old moose
into any old woods*

*but watch where you step!*

## Day after Day

you take the elevator
to the second floor

where you pick up
*The New York Times*

but today you stop
and ask, *is it*

*on the first floor or*
*second?*

## Expectations

He makes me repeat
  every dumb thing
    I say as if
      he expects
        me to be a s
          i
           m
            u
            l
             t
             a
              n
               e
                 o
                  u
                    s
                      interpreter
                      at the U.N.,
                      and I can't
                      bear it.

# Getting It Right

He shuts
windows
I open.

I open
windows
he shuts.

I propose
there be a
mandatory

thermo-
dynamic
assessment,

before any two
people get married.

## Ready Made

  I used to
  j o k e  I
  m a r r i e d
  y o u  f o r
   your legs,
   dancer's
    l e g s,
   e v e n
   today,
  a f t e r
these
many
many
years,
 slender
 and shapely.

# Metamorphosis

Kafka's *Metamorphosis*
lay open on the bed.

*Would I like it?* asks the Old Man.

I read the opening sentence aloud:

> When Gregor Samsa woke up
> one morning from unsettling dreams,
> he found himself changed
> in his bed to a monstrous vermin.

I flip forward a few pages.

> For in fact, day by day,
> he saw things less distinctly.

*Would I like it?*

## Quandary

Sometimes I
    ask myself,
were he
    to be
taken away
    tomorrow,
would I
    weep
a sigh
    of relief,
or would I
    weep for
how he
    used to be?

# Each Morning

before I rise,
  I glance
     over at
      his side
      of the bed
      and watch
     the covers
    rise and fall
   and know
   there
  will
  be
  o
   n
    e

      m
     o
     r
    e

    d
    a
    y.

# Part 2

## How It Happened

The Old Man reaches for a stamp
that fluttered onto our blue
flowered carpet.

And as if he were as light
as that stamp, he falls.
Stefan, at my computer,
dashes over to where
he lies. Lifts him
back onto
his chair.

The Old Man blinks.
It will take him a
few minutes
to forget.

## Déjà Vu

Our daughter
shops at Ikea for

a plaid duvet,
a lamp and a chair
for her father's room
at memory care.

Was it only last year
she shopped
at Ikea for

the same sorts of
things for her daughter's
college dorm room.

# The Time Comes

1.
Your head bobs. You fall asleep
listening to *The News Hour*, *The Good Wife*,
or reading a new poem of mine.

You stop picking up the mail, and even if
it's warm and sunny, you will no longer
walk around the pond.

You are a wreck every time I leave,
Each day now bad things happen.
The time has come.

2.
So where do YOU sleep? you ask.
Upstairs in MY bed.
(I'm careful not to say OUR bed.)

I leave during a geriatric sing along.
Tremulous voices singing, *Oh Susanna,*
don't you cry for me.

# First Day

We move his favorite tchotchkes,
his favorite family pictures,
his favorite photograph
albums, his stamps,
though he can't tell
which countries
they belong to.
Our daughter
takes him to
arts and crafts,
where they each
paint a flower with
a bright yellow center.
With scissors, they
cut out floppy
white petals.

I tape the flowers to the outside
of his door, so he will know
which room is his.

## Three Monkeys

Our daughter, our granddaughter, and our son-in-law
stop by memory care so our granddaughter
can say goodbye. Tomorrow, at the crack of dawn,
she goes to college and won't be back till Christmas.

(Will he still recognize her?
Will he still be alive?)

The three sit on the Old Man's bed.
The two of us stare at the three of them.

I have a flashback of those three famous monkeys
at Nikko's *Tochigi* shrine: see no evil,
hear no evil, speak no evil.

Our son-in-law rubs our granddaughter's back;
our granddaughter rubs her mom's back;
our daughter rubs no one's back.

*Hey,* I shout. *What about me?*

Like those three monkeys,
one does not hear me; one
does not see me; but
one leaps off the bed
and rubs my back.

## Now and Then

Something we love
doing together
is to browse through
old photograph albums.

I open up one on Japan
dating back to when
we first moved there.

Here you are, kicking off your skis.
By it, you wrote: *never again
a family ski weekend.*

Here I am, guzzling *sake*,
after too long a sail
on Sagami bay.

Here is our daughter at eight,
looking like a Japanese doll,
about to perform
at our neighborhood festival.

Here is our long-haired son, scowling.
The last thing he needs is me, taking his picture.

## Interpretation

You walk up
to this man
who stands there
c o m a t o s e
and ask, *are you
m e d i t a t i n g?*
and I whisper,
*more likely, he
is vegetating.*

# When I Least Expect It

he's rushed
by ambulance
to the ER.

Hooked onto
a bag of
intravenous
antibiotics
and fluids.

His temperature spikes
to a hundred and four.

## Odd

We hire
a sitter who
has on the
inside of his
right forearm
a tattoo in
indigo blue:
*Mother*
on a tombstone.

## The Good News

is that he is beginning
to eat a little, and with
verbal cues, he can
get up out of bed.

Yesterday, I took him
into the garden where,
under the shade of
an unidentifiable tree,
shaped like a lollipop,

he nibbled on pretzels
and slices of watermelon.

# Phone Call

Tonight he had the night nurse
put in a call to me.

*Where are you?*
*Why aren't you*
*here with me?*

I say, *yesterday, I took you in for a haircut*
*and a beard trim, so now no one*
*will mistake you for a werewolf.*

*Was that you?* he asks.
*I thought it was*
*someone else.*

*Tell me. I need to know.*
*Where is it that you*
*and my mother sleep?*

## Broken Record

Her two front teeth missing,
Ella staggers into his room.

*Hi…hi.. hi…honey.*
*Do you remember?*
*Do you remember?*
*Do you remember?*

*What can I do?*
*What can I do?*
*What can I do?*

*How do I get home?*
*How do I get home?*
*How do I get home?*

*I gotta get home.*
*I gotta get home.*
*I gotta get home.*

*Do you remember?*
*Do you remember?*
*Do you remember?*

*What can I do?*
*What can I do?*
*What can I do?*

As if she were some sort of push toy,
an aide guides her out the door.

## Manuela

Eighty-five year old Manuela
glances at her watch.

*My mother and my father are due any minute.*

*I wonder which one will drive?*
*My mother says my father*
*is way too old to drive, but*
*she lets him drive anyway.*
*She doesn't want to risk*
*upsetting him.*

An aide rolls her eyes, *Lord, save me from getting old.*

## Half a Sandwich

He stares down at a bowl of soup,
half a sandwich, a box
of high protein fruit drink,
and a dixie cup
of high nutrient ice cream.

Slowly, oh so slowly, he eats and sips
through a straw, while I fidget
in my chair, imagining
the poem I might
write tonight.

Manuela grabs her purse, sweater and book.
She waves goodbye again. After all,
it is a long walk to Puerto Rico.

## Manuela is Told the Truth

*Yesterday this mean man burst into my room and said,*

*my mother and father*
*are dead! Dead—*
*can you imagine?*
*He's crazy!*
*He's out*
*of his mind!*

*My father and grandfather are due any minute.*

## Just Kidding
*First line from Shakespeare's Sonnet 110*

"Alas, 'tis true I've gone here and there."
A stream's current is seldom still.
And yet I declare it unfair
Of you to expect me to stay until
The yawn of each day's sameness
Makes backyard birds go mute.

Let all the whys and wherefores
Be nameless for it is beyond refute
Dry cheeks attest to tears unshed.
Before leaping off a bridge, I'd
Sooner take off on my own instead
Of remain cowering at your side.

It is easier to remake a life than to build
Upon a thirst and hunger unfulfilled.

## Identity Theft

Because mid-sentence
he loses track
of whatever
it is he is
trying to say.

Because I don't
want to think
about what
comes next.

Because I am
ashamed to admit
the ear of my heart
is no longer listening.

## Enigma

Loving someone
even though
you are well
a w a r e
that his
sense of
w h a t  is
is skewed,
is the same as
p l a y i n g  a
g a m e  o f
f o l l o w
the dots
without
a single dot
to  follow.

## Fun House Mirror

Be wary, my love.
A fun house mirror
distorts what is
into what isn't.

You, my modern day
King Lear, stumble across
a rough and threatening terrain.

I rack my brain
for a way to make
it easier for you.

All I can manage to do
is visit you each day.

# Notes

Reference is made to the following authors and works:

Epigraph: Wallace Stevens, excerpt from "Of Modern Poetry," in *The Collected Poems of Wallace Stevens* (Alfred A. Knopf, 1990), page 239.

OCD: Obsessive Compulsive Disorder.

"Metamorphosis": Franz Kafka, excerpt from *The Metamorphosis,* trans. S. Bernofsky (W.W. Norton & Company, 2014), p. 34.

"Just Kidding": William Shakespeare, excerpt from "Sonnet 110," in *The Complete Sonnets and Poems* (Oxford University Press, 2002).

Printed in the United States
By Bookmasters